Ana's Birthday

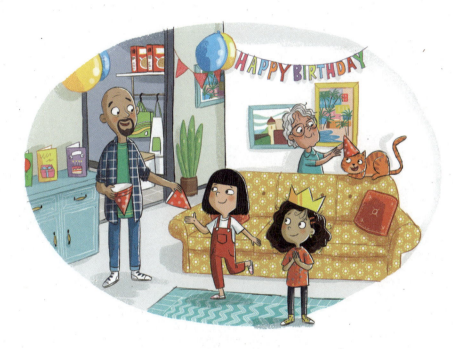

by Angela Báez • illustrated by Gareth Conway

Lucy Calkins and Michael Rae-Grant, Series Editors

LETTER-SOUND CORRESPONDENCES
m, t, a, n, s, ss, p, i, d, g, o, c, k, ck, r, u, h

HIGH-FREQUENCY WORDS
is, like, see, the, no, so, **has**, **his**

Ana's Birthday
Author: Angela Báez
Series Editors: Lucy Calkins and Michael Rae-Grant

Heinemann
145 Maplewood Avenue, Suite 300
Portsmouth, NH 03801
www.heinemann.com

Copyright © 2023 Heinemann and The Reading and Writing Project Network, LLC

All rights reserved, including but not limited to the right to reproduce this book, or portions thereof, in any form or by any means whatsoever, without written permission from the publisher. For information on permission for reproductions or subsidiary rights licensing, please contact Heinemann at permissions@heinemann.com. Heinemann's authors have devoted their entire careers to developing the unique content in their works, and their written expression is protected by copyright law. We respectfully ask that you do not adapt, reuse, or copy anything on third-party (whether for-profit or not-for-profit) lesson-sharing websites.
—Heinemann Publishers

"Dedicated to Teachers" is a trademark of Greenwood Publishing Group, LLC.

Cataloging-in-Publication data is on file with the Library of Congress.

ISBN-13: 978-0-325-13800-8

Design and Production: Dinardo Design LLC, Carole Berg, and Rebecca Anderson

Editors: Anna Cockerille and Jennifer McKenna

Illustrations: Gareth Conway

Photographs: p. 32 © Monkey Business Images/Shutterstock; inside back cover (hat) © montego/Shutterstock; inside back cover (sock) © Pakhnyushchy/Shutterstock.

Manufacturing: Gerard Clancy

Printed in the United States of America on acid-free paper
2 3 4 5 6 7 8 9 10 MP 28 27 26 25 24 23 22
November 2022 Printing / PO# 34910

Contents

1. Dad and Ana Spin 1
2. The Window Is Stuck 13
3. Ana's Birthday 23

Meet...

Ana

Dad

Pip

Abuela

Tam

Dad and Ana Spin

Dad has the music on, and I run in.

I tap Dad,
and Dad grins.

I snap and hum.

Dad rocks his hips.

I skip and hop.

Dad and I spin…

and spin...

and spin...

and SMACK!
Dad and I hit the window!

Dad trips and…

UG!

Dad is on his rump.

And I hug him!

The Window Is Stuck

It is hot, hot, hot.
Hot like the sun.

And the window is stuck!

Dad tugs at the window.

Pip pats at the window.

I hit the window.

Dad is hot, hot, hot.
So Dad picks up his rag.

Pip is hot, hot, hot.
So Pip has a sip.

I am hot, hot, hot.
So I ram the window!

And the window is NOT stuck!

Pip and I sit in the window.
Dad hums to the music.
And it is not so hot!

Ana's Birthday

It is Ana's birthday!
Dad has hats.

And Dad has a stick
so the kids and Pip can play.

Ana hits it,
Tam hits it,
and Abuela hits it.

Pip hops up and...

Pip hits it. POP!
Pip got it!

Dad hands Ana a sack and grins.

Drums!

Like Dad's drums!

Birthday music!

> Learn about...

PIÑATAS

If a piñata (pin-ya-ta) is hanging up, you know it's time for a celebration! *Piñatas* are made out of colorful paper and cardboard, and they come in lots of different shapes and sizes. Some look like animals, some look like stars, and some even look like famous characters from movies or TV.

Piñatas are *hollow*, which means they're empty inside. That's so they can get filled up with candy, small toys, or other treats. Once it's full of treats, the piñata is hung from a string, and then people take turns hitting it with a stick until it breaks open. Sometimes you wear a blindfold when you try to hit the piñata, which makes it extra tricky!

When the piñata bursts open, all the treats fall to the ground, and people rush to gather them. Piñatas are fun to play with at a birthday party or at any kind of celebration!

> Talk about...

Ask your reader some questions like...

- What happened in this book?
- Why were Ana, Dad, and Pip so hot? How did opening the window help?
- What did Ana get for her birthday? Did she like it? Why?
- Have you celebrated a birthday before? How was your celebration the same as Ana's? How was it different?